YOU ARE

Worthy

OF

NEW

BEGINNINGS

STEPPING FORWARD WITH FAITH
AND ENDLESS POSSIBILITIES

MYA CYNTHIA JOHNSON

You Are Worthy of New Beginnings

Stepping Forward with Faith and Endless Possibilities

Book Design by Transcendent Publishing

Editing by Mary Rembert

ISBN: 979-8-9935722-5-3

And here you are living despite it all.

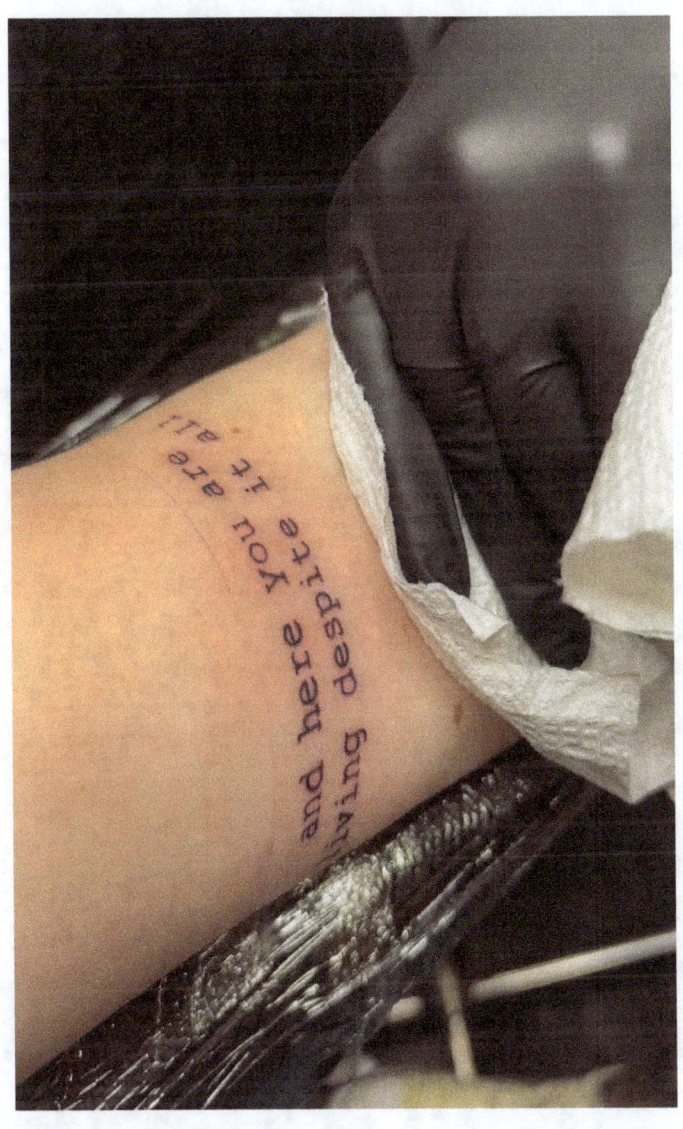

Table of Contents

Dedication

I dedicate this book to my village, who have steadfastly supported me. To my mom, who always believed in me and never wavered in her faith. To my dad, who constantly encouraged me to strive for the best version of myself. To the friends and family who lifted me up and extended their arms when I needed them most, rather than turning away. To my Heavenly Father, thank you for walking beside me, carrying me through the darkest valleys, and continually working in my life to turn all things into good.

Get Off the Floor, You Have Living to Do

I didn't grow up imagining I'd become the girl who mastered the art of holding herself together in public. Yet here I am, smiling on cue, cracking jokes, and carrying myself like someone who never trembles. But inside? My foot dances under the table, my leg shakes without my permission, and half the time I'm just trying to breathe steadily. Compliments make me look down at the floor, not because I'm shy, but because I'm busy arguing with the voice in my head that tells me I don't deserve them.

I've always been able to see the beauty in other people: their strength, their worth, their goodness. Mine? I've had a harder time finding it. Lately, the weight of my mistakes presses on my chest, and I wonder if I'll ever grow into the woman I keep picturing: calm, confident, certain of who she is. I thought I'd be further along by now. I really did. And sometimes when I look back, I see moments I didn't take, doors I didn't walk through, and I blame myself for things I shouldn't have carried.

Somewhere in the logical part of my mind, I know I am loved. I know I matter. I know God didn't rush when He created me. But those truths don't always settle into my heart, into the place where belief becomes identity.

On too many days, I feel bruised by life, worn down, disappointed in myself. I wrestle with the idea that I should be ahead by now, that everyone else is sprinting while I'm stumbling. But even that, especially that, is part of my story.

The truth is, I've lived through things that should have leveled me. Losses that hollowed me out, nights where I wondered if I'd make it to morning, shame so heavy it felt like a second skin. And yet … I didn't break. God kept me breathing. God kept me here. I am living proof that the moments we think will finish us often end up becoming the chapters that testify to God's protection.

That's why I'm finally ready to say this out loud: being human is messy. It always has been. But it's also holy, because it gives God room to work. There is nothing wrong with being imperfect. There is nothing wrong with falling apart before you learn how to rise. Everything you need—strength, healing, confidence, purpose—already exists inside you. It's been waiting beneath the noise of self-doubt and the heavy armor of self-criticism. Waiting for you to loosen your grip and let Him in.

My mom always told me, "Get off the floor, sweetheart. You have living to do." And maybe that's why you're here. Maybe something in you is tired of crawling. Perhaps you're ready—scared, but ready—for a fresh beginning.

I know what it's like to feel lost, alone, hopeless, and convinced there's no place for you. I've been there. In one of those moments, God nudged my mom to send me an email with a simple message and a link—an unexpected lifeline. That tiny act cracked something open in me. It made me whisper a tiny prayer I didn't know I needed: God, show me a different way.

I've walked through trauma, heartbreak, betrayal, and pain that left long shadows. But at 20 years old, I made a decision: I wanted to heal. Not halfway. Not when it was convenient. I wanted to become a peaceful, healthy version of myself—the one I knew God kept trying to lead me toward. And that choice changed everything.

Maybe you're reading this because you need someone who understands. Maybe you're a parent trying to understand a child's journey with mental health. Maybe you're here because you're ready to start your own healing. Whoever you are, you've picked up this book for a reason. I believe God brought you to these pages the same way He brought me to mine: through a gentle nudge, a moment of honesty, or maybe even desperation.

Healing isn't a single decision; it's a daily commitment. I tried therapy, medication, all the "right" things—but healing didn't start working until I wanted it more than I wanted the familiar comfort of my pain. Only you can choose your beginning. Only you can walk toward it. But you don't walk alone.

I've restarted this introduction so many times, waiting for the perfect opening line, the perfect tone, the perfect words. But nothing about healing is perfect. Nothing about life is perfect. And maybe that's precisely why now is the right time. Because I'm not writing from the finish line, I'm writing from the middle. From a place where God is still working, still shaping, still restoring.

This book is my journey toward new beginnings, toward faith, healing, courage, and the quiet rediscovery of who God created me to be.

I hope that as I share my story, you'll start to uncover your own because you are worthy of the life still waiting for you.

The Weight I Carried: Before the Healing Began

I have always dreamed of who I want to become and the steps I would need to take to get there. I just didn't think it would be this hard. It seemed like every time I took a step forward toward finally being okay and getting to this person I felt so strongly about being, I would hit rock bottom again. There were circumstances beyond my control, but at times, I did not handle them properly. I was not helping me become the me I had dreamed of being.

This is considered a self-help book, but it is more of an autobiography about my journey. If you picked up this book, you've probably had some of the same experiences I've had, but even if you haven't, I truly believe that hearing my story will help you. Hearing different perspectives and learning how someone else overcame a challenge can help you or a loved one, as you never know what life will throw your way.

What took me so long to start my true healing journey was that I had no hope for myself. Maybe you are feeling the same way. Maybe you really want to be and feel better, but you have no idea where to start or how to truly dedicate yourself to it.

I am going to be honest; it is hard to find true dedication when things seem impossible, or you are at rock bottom. There are many sacrifices that one must make to be truly dedicated to healing. I am very lucky in the sense that I had other people make extreme sacrifices to help me find my journey to becoming the adult I yearned to be.

I had to put a lot of my life on pause. That meant leaving school, friends, activities, etc., to go back home and start my specific journey. What I was doing and what I had done were not working for me. I wasn't going to therapy regularly, and I wasn't consistently staying on my medications. I wasn't doing anything to truly help myself.

For as long as I can remember, people have told me I will do something great. I never believed them. How could they possibly know? It seemed that everywhere I went, someone felt something after meeting me. It was very strange to me, but since I started my healing journey, I have begun to believe that I am capable of something great and I am worthy of love.

That is the power of healing from the inside out, being compassionate with yourself, self-love, and taking your healing into your own hands. I am not sure what I am supposed to do, but I am slowly finding my purpose, and you are capable of that too.

Let's be real; everyone has been through a lot. Everyone has been through hardships and different circumstances, and I am here to tell you I can relate. I not only relate to it, but I am also angry about it and have all these hard feelings about everything I have been through. It is so easy for someone to be positive in a situation. And let me tell you, when someone tells me to just be positive, I get so rattled because I feel like they don't understand. It is okay to be angry, sad, upset, or confused; emotions are not only okay but essential. Feel them. Write down how they make you feel.

In the moment, it is so hard to see the good in a situation with challenging circumstances or difficult situations, so feel those emotions and let them release. Releasing emotions can be healing. If you let them sit too long, they get buried deep down and cause other symptoms. Let them out into the open. Ask God to take these emotions and help you through them. Cry, laugh, scream, anything you need to do to set them free so you can start healing.

The key to this is not to let yourself stay there too long. This may sound a bit cliché, and I acknowledge that it is, but remember, everything happens for a reason, you could also say purpose. Your hurt will become glory one day, and you will be able to help so many other people who have gone through what you have gone through, but that doesn't necessarily make it okay.

I remember being mad at God because of everything I have been through at such a young age. I got Lyme disease as a child, and it was not diagnosed for two and a half years. I was really upset about being sick as a child, and what helped me was that one day, I remember my mom telling me, "God gives his hardest battles to his strongest warriors." That stuck with me. It reminded me that I am strong and capable of doing hard things. Yes, be mad, be sad, but remember you are going through this for a reason and that you are strong. Trust me, I know it is hard to stay positive in certain situations, and it's infuriating to hear someone say that. Feel your feelings, and remember you are going to do glorious things.

As I said, everyone has been through a lot, but here is a glimpse into my story. At the age of 13, I started having weird health symptoms. I ended up having Lyme disease, but it went undiagnosed for many, many years and changed my entire life. I still have deficits from it to this day.

I have lost so many family members that I am close to; I even found my uncle dead on the floor at a very young age. I have had sexual and emotional trauma, and I probably will not dive very much into that part because it can be very triggering to people, but I just want to let you know that if you are dealing with sexual assault, trauma, or things around those lines, I understand the guilt and pain that you feel.

At age 20, I had a stroke, and there was so much medical trauma and mistreatment that it is hard for me to trust doctors and the medical system. I have battled with suicide and mental health disease, so it can be hard to do day-to-day things.

But here I am, telling my story, and telling YOU that you can do it. You can also be a happy, healthy, peace-filled, functioning adult if you so desire. I understand, and I am here for you.

God uses circumstances in life to provoke faith. It can be your most amazing opportunities or your most tragic losses. Things are not unintentional; God has a plan, everything happens for a reason, and everything provokes faith. It took me a long time to think about life in this way. Everything we do should be while we walk in faith. We are not alone. God is there, holding our hand every step of the way, and He has a plan for us. It is hard, and I am definitely guilty of this, to truly let go and know God is in control. I always try to control every outcome and every aspect of my life. I have a hard time letting go. I need to put my trust in God always. We can all work on this; no one is perfect at it. It is difficult to understand why terrible things happen, but without those hardships I have faced, I would not be able to understand people as well as I do, and I would not be writing my story right now.

The Weight I Carried:
Before the Healing Began

  What are you hoping to get out of this book?

_____

_____

_____

  Is it for you?

_____

_____

_____

  Is it for someone else?

_____

_____

_____

  What hardships have you endured in your life that you need healing from?

_____

_____

_____

_____

The Breaking Point and Learning How to Heal Again

*B*efore I talk about what really worked for me, I will tell you all the things I tried that did not work and even sometimes made things worse. I have tried so many different types of therapy: talk therapy, equine therapy, etc. I have also gone to inpatient facilities for a more aggressive approach.

I have tried med after med and seen different therapists and psychiatrists, but it seems that I couldn't find something that worked well enough so that I didn't have to do anything myself. I felt beaten down, depressed, and hopeless. I thought that I had let all my trauma and circumstances get in the way of my happiness, and I punished myself for it every single day.

Therapy is always a good place to start. It kept me somewhat stable for many years. What I did not like about talk therapy was that I felt like I was rehashing everything over and over with no real solution. Talking about my feelings is very important, but that's all I thought I was doing for years. Yes, it helped me reach a baseline of steady emotions for a little while, but it only lasted for so long. After rehashing every emotion I felt over and over, I eventually hit rock bottom. I would come back up and hit rock bottom again; it wasn't working for me.

I saw many psychiatrists who gave me different diagnoses, but the overall consistent recommendation was that I needed medication. I tried so many different medications, and the problem with this process is that you have to be on the medication that you are prescribed for at least six weeks to see if it is truly working or not. I had meds that made things so much worse, ones that made me cry all the time and feel more depressed, anxious, and even suicidal. Not every medication works for everyone, and it is basically a trial-and-error process.

You also have to be on the medications consistently. It messes everything up, even if you just miss a dose or two, and that is what really beat me down.

I was in high school when I started taking medication for my mental health, and I felt like I was the only one who had mental health struggles that required medication. I did not want to take pills every day; I felt different, or I just forgot. There were a lot of lame excuses that I made up in my head for why I was not going to take my medication.

My parents have always had my back. They have never given up on me, no matter how hard things have been in life or with me. I had a suicide attempt when I went home because I felt hopeless and that I was not deserving of anything. It landed me in the ICU, and that's when they knew I needed something other than just therapy and medication.

My mom did research nonstop and came across physicians using ketamine to rewire the brain for people with things such as severe anxiety, depression, PTSD, and so much more. There just so happened to be a place in my hometown that had had extreme success. Thankfully, I was able to get a consultation and then eventually get cleared for ketamine treatment. I knew that just doing the ketamine was not going to be enough; I was going to have to work hard in processing my trauma and working to do things to help with my anxiety.

Eventually, after deciding to dedicate myself to healing, I found the right regimen of medications. I also found an amazing therapist who has helped me through so much and has helped me get to where I am today.

You have to stick with it and not give up. You will find the right course of meds and the right therapist; it just takes time. Don't get discouraged. Remember, your time is coming.

This was the turning point in my journey because, for the first time, I could see a glimpse of hope and a glimmer of light at the end of a very dark tunnel, and I was finally ready to put in the work.

This health center, where I would see a psychiatrist, a doctor, and a therapist, finally put me at peace. I remember walking in, having that first appointment, and knowing deep down and in my heart that this was where I would get the help I needed.

It was refreshing to actually feel heard by physicians, and I knew they wanted to help. I was able to be open and honest, and they listened. I got cleared for ketamine treatments after a couple of sessions, and this approach changed my life. I put in a lot of work, but without the ketamine, I do not think I would have truly been able to work through my deep-rooted trauma.

I am not saying this approach is for everyone. I felt like my family and I had exacerbated every measure to help me. This, to me, was my last hope. It may seem extreme, but after researching and talking about outcomes, I knew it was the approach for me.

Ketamine can truly uproot deep-rooted trauma. It is not always pleasant. Sometimes, you have to sit through unpleasant journeys to see a new light; sometimes, the journey is amazing, and you get to see people you love or miss so dearly.

Whatever it is, you have to let God take your hand and trust that He will guide you on the journey you are meant to have. Seeing trauma, instead of just talking about it, can help people talk about what is really bothering them or why it was so traumatic for them.

When I talk about a ketamine journey, I am talking about the experiences you experience while you are on the medicine. You are in a different state of mind, a psychedelic state where reality is altered. Ketamine therapy takes place in a clinical setting, and you have a calm environment, a therapist, music, and anything you need to make yourself comfortable to get the most out of your journey with the medicine.

Ketamine can do some pretty remarkable things. It does not work on serotonin or dopamine; it works on different parts of your brain to get the best result for your mental health. My ketamine was administered through an IV for dosing control reasons. The journey or experience took effect in about 10 minutes and lasted 45 minutes to an hour. I couldn't control what I was going to experience or what I was going to see, but I would always invite God and my loved ones in to protect me and help me heal.

Everyone's experience with ketamine is different. I am lucky that I got to reunite with family members and have vivid journeys. Some people only see black, some see shapes and colors, and for some, it is not very enjoyable. I am one of the ones who had a very specific experience, and everyone's journey will be different.

Moments of Reflection

❧ What things have you tried in the past to help with your mental health?

_____

_____

_____

_____

_____

_____

❧ Were they beneficial?

_____

_____

_____

_____

_____

❧ Are there other approaches you would like to try?

_____

_____

_____

_____

_____

_____

Rephrasing The "Why": Strengthening Your Faith

I often find myself asking God, "Why?" Why do people get taken away from us, get cancer, or go through horrible things? Why?

I found my answer, but it is not an answer to the why. I had to rephrase the question to God and not doubt him. I had to repent my sins and trust in him always.

God always has a plan, so completely surrender to Him and let His plan take action. Live as God would want you to by being kind, loving, compassionate, and understanding. God is the only thing you can always count on, and knowing that will truly save you.

I remember I was having a really tough night. Most nights are tough for me mentally, but this one was especially so. I was confused, upset, and maybe even a little mad.

Luckily, my mom was in Mississippi visiting me at college, and we had a long talk. It seemed as if these emotions about my faith were supposed to come over me while she was there. My mom has a very special relationship with God, one I hope to have with Him one day as well. She and I spent hours talking about my feelings, and she told me there was something she wanted me to watch.

She sent me a clip, and I recognized the person immediately. She told me God was telling her that this was the message I needed to hear. The person in the video was my step-uncle, but I consider that whole side of the family my blood; I don't like to use the word step as family is family to me.

My uncle and his sister, whom I never got to meet, were in a terrible accident. They were hiking Little Bear Peak in Colorado when an avalanche hit, and his sister was tragically taken. My uncle was interviewed, and I was unaware of this interview until my mom sent it to me. My uncle found himself asking God why something this terrible would happen. My whole life, I have been doing the same thing, asking why I was beaten down over and over and had so many setbacks.

Asking God why is an unanswerable question. We don't get to know the "why"; instead, we need to trust in Him that there is a reason behind everything, even if that reason is not clear in the moment. We need to repent in the moment, not our sins, but repent for doubting God.

God does everything in the course that is best for your life. He is faithful and will always be there for you, but you need to rephrase your "why."

I had a hard time grasping what my uncle said in his interview. I had to dive into it with God myself to truly grasp this concept. I realize the "why" might be beyond human understanding or even acceptance. God's presence is the answer to every question. Matthew 7:7 says, "Ask, and you will receive, seek, and you will find, knock, and the door will be opened to you."

When you turn to God and surrender, and I mean completely and truly surrender to Him, you will not be let down. His presence is the answer to every question and will save you. I like to look at all the hardships and losses as God teaching me something for the greater good. If you had told me that everything I was going through had a purpose, I would have thought you were crazy. Now, I know all those hardships and lessons were for my purpose: to help people and make a difference.

God's way is not always our way. I would not have chosen all the pain and suffering I have gone through. Turning to God can settle your doubts and give you peace in your situation. I am still working on a stronger relationship with God, but I know that when I turn to Him and give myself completely to Him, I get clarity and peace.

Questioning God is not a sin. It helps us clarify his will and his ways, even if we don't completely and utterly understand them. Questioning God is an invitation to grow closer to him and to strengthen your faith as well.

My uncle was so deeply hurt by the death of his sister. Anybody would be. He did not get his question of "why" answered, but he did learn to turn to God, and it strengthened their relationship. Remember, God always has a will and a way. Trust and surrender to Him, and remember his plan is for the greater good.

I decided to interview my uncle to get a deeper understanding of his grief and his relationship with God. When my uncle came off that mountain after the avalanche, he was in the hospital alone for a long time because there was no one around, and it took some time for his family to get to him.

Sitting in the hospital, he said to God, "God, I don't know what just happened to me. What just happened doesn't align with my worldview of you." He continued to ask why this happened. He was pleading with God to know why.

God decided to take him back to the Bible. He was reading Job at the time, and a little backstory about Job is that terrible things kept happening to him. Through everything, he kept asking God the question, "Why?" Job wanted to know what he had done wrong to deserve all of these terrible life-changing events that were happening to him. God would say that he never said he did anything wrong, but Job kept asking unanswerable questions, and God would always respond that he is God.

Do you know God or not? Are you hearing or seeing God? Once you have seen him, it doesn't matter what has happened. My uncle still knows God; he has seen the remarkable things that God can do. He repented that he questioned His righteousness or His truth.

My uncle said, "If I can see who you are, this will be okay. If I can see you, I know everything will be okay." He explained to me that from eternity's perspective, his sister is in a better place. Whenever he turns to God, He shows him unbelievable things about him and his family. None of it makes it okay, but what makes it better is that he knows God better. The plans he chooses for us are higher and greater than the ones we would have chosen for ourselves.

When you are struggling to know why something happened, turn to God and let him show you that he is real and with you. Ask God who he is and ask him to tell you something about Himself today.

God will be faithful in answering in different ways, and he will always show you that he is there. If you ask, "God, who are you?" you will get an unbelievable response. Remember, he is always with you and has a gorgeous plan for your life.

After talking with my uncle, I had a better understanding of how to approach God in difficult times. Simply using prayer and asking Him to show me who He is has helped me deal with difficult situations, nights of severe anxiety, and losing loved ones. Turn to God; He will not let you down. I have learned so much about myself by doing this.

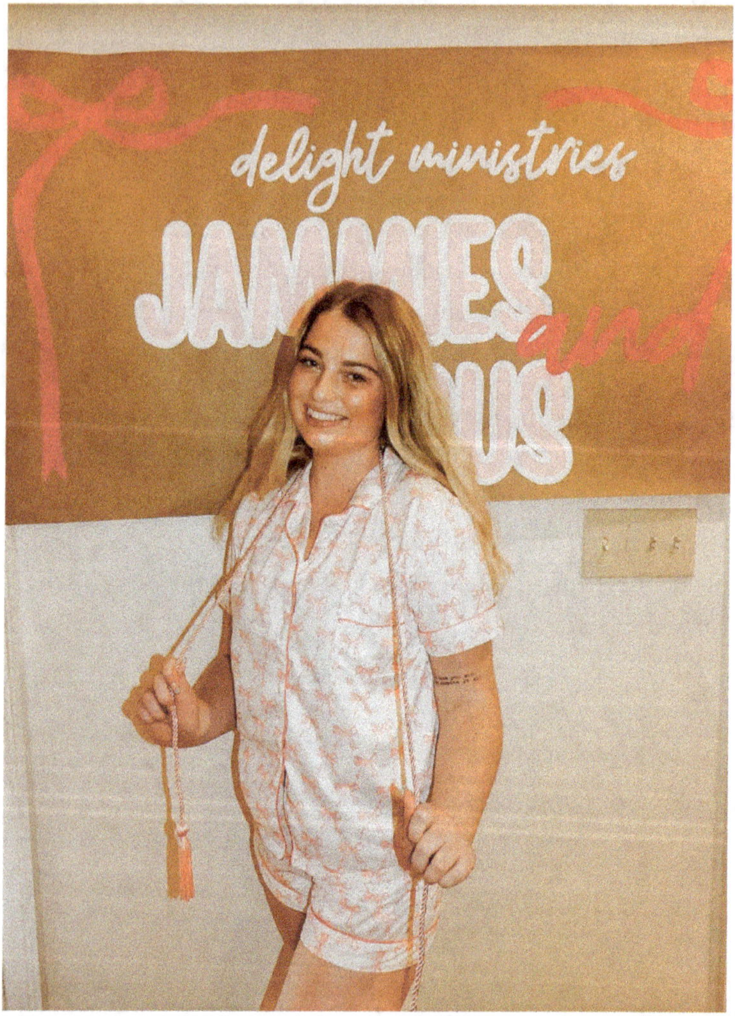

Moments of Reflection

✍ Has there ever been a time when you turned to God and asked him why something was happening? If so, how can you rephrase your "Why?"

_____

_____

_____

_____

_____

_____

_____

_____

_____

✍ How can you turn to God and trust that he is there?

_____

_____

_____

_____

_____

_____

_____

_____

_____

_____

_____

_____

Riding the Waves:
Currents of Closure

I have had anxiety for as long as I can remember. It started in 2011 when my grandfather, whom I called Popi, unexpectedly passed away in his sleep at a very young age. I was young, but I vividly remember how shocked everyone was and how many people needed to grieve his death because he had such a lasting impact on so many people. I was eight years old, and to experience a loss like that and see the people around me change because of it was very traumatic.

Everyone experiences loss and grief, but having to understand and feel loss at that young age was shocking. I am honestly surprised that I remember it all so vividly. I had just been with him a couple of weeks before, and then he was suddenly gone. This kickstarted my avalanche of anxiety that grew and grew over the years, and little did I know I would experience grief and loss over and over again in the years to come.

One thing about ketamine is you never know where your journey is going to take you. You must have no expectations, but at the same time, have great expectations. You can never force yourself to have a specific journey or see someone you want to see. You have to just be and remember: no expectations, great expectations.

Before each session, I would invite God and loved ones to take me on the journey I needed to go on and to show me the message I was meant to see. You have to be as curious as a kid. Explore whatever you see, and let the journey take you wherever you are supposed to go.

Feeling the sand on my toes, the warm Florida breeze on my face, and hearing the crashing of the waves in the ocean, I immediately knew who I would see once the ketamine journey began. And there he was, my Popi, as happy and go-lucky as I remembered. Tears started flowing because I had missed him so much. I immediately felt unexplainable gratitude that this was going to be my ketamine journey.

I was young, but I knew exactly what family trip to Florida he was bringing me back to. I could see the purple-striped bathing suit I was wearing and all my family that was there. We were building sand castles and laughing while having a great day at the beach.

My Popi signaled me to follow him into the ocean. I followed, hoping the message I needed to know would be clear. There was no talking involved, but I knew he was there with me, trying to tell me something I needed to do to release all of the trauma I had experienced from his death. Then we were on a boat. I'm not sure how we got there, but hey, it's ketamine; things don't have to make sense.

We were on a boat riding the waves in the ocean, and I looked at my Popi, and he was just being. Being still. Being in the moment and taking everything in. I knew he was trying to show me how to just be, which is something I struggle with. I always want to be a human doing, not a human being. He was trying to show me to be more stress-free and just ride the waves of life. I started crying again because he believed I could be the person I yearned to be, the attributes I saw in him that I wanted to see in myself.

We arrived at our destination, and I knew exactly where we were. We were at a beautiful cemetery in Florida, and I knew this was where my Popi was buried. He brought me to his gravestone and stood there, once again practicing being still and in the moment.

He smiled and pointed at it as if something was there waiting for me. I couldn't make out what the headstone said, but I knew he was trying to tell me there was a message for me. I started coming out of the medicine and needed to process what he was trying to tell me.

After processing and thinking, I said to my therapist, "I think I need to go to Miami and see my Popi's grave. There is something there waiting for me, and I think it will give me closure." My ketamine journey had taken me to a specific place, and I felt at peace that that was where I needed to go and be to truly heal the hole I felt in my body deep down. My ketamine journey turned into an actual physical journey to Miami to get the closure I needed.

I shared my ketamine journey with my dad. My Popi was his dad, and I told him, "You changed when Popi died. I feel like I lost a part of you." He stopped for a moment and started thinking. My dad is not the type to open up, but what he said to me next definitely made us closer and gave me even more closure. He explained that the loss was hard. Any loss of a parent or loved one is always going to be difficult, but he explained that he and his dad were just starting to build a different kind of relationship, and he missed out on building it to see where it would go. My dad sharing that with me was very personal. It made us closer and gave me a better understanding of grief, that part where you continue to go through life without your loved one. That gave me more closure because I understood my dad better, bringing us closer together.

Closure might not be what you always think it is, but going to Miami, doing something that reminded me of the good times with my Popi, and getting closer to my dad was all the closure I needed. That helped me work past my trauma of losing my Popi. It took 13 years for it to come, but it finally did.

When I went to visit the grave on my Popi's death date, something really stood out to me. On his stone, it said "beloved by all." That was the word I was looking for. He was beloved by all.

I remember standing there in the pouring rain, crying and trying to understand why God would take away someone so beloved. We may not always understand, but God does not choose others because they are more worthy or they praise him more. God is always in control, and we need to trust in him and know that there is always a plan. I believe that losing someone is a mystery of divine will. I believe that God's ways can be beyond human understanding because, as I was standing over my Popi's grave, I felt peace. It was thundering and lightning, but everything went quiet. It was as if he were calming my mind. Calming me in the sense that not everything has to make sense at this moment and time; I could just be. I was standing there, soaking wet, trying to understand why he was taken away, but God was telling me I may never fully understand and to trust the process he has for us.

I will remember that day forever. I honored him by getting a special tattoo of a poppy flower in remembrance of my Popi. Honoring him with this flower will always be something I have. It makes me feel closer to him and reminds me how blessed I am to have known such a beloved person.

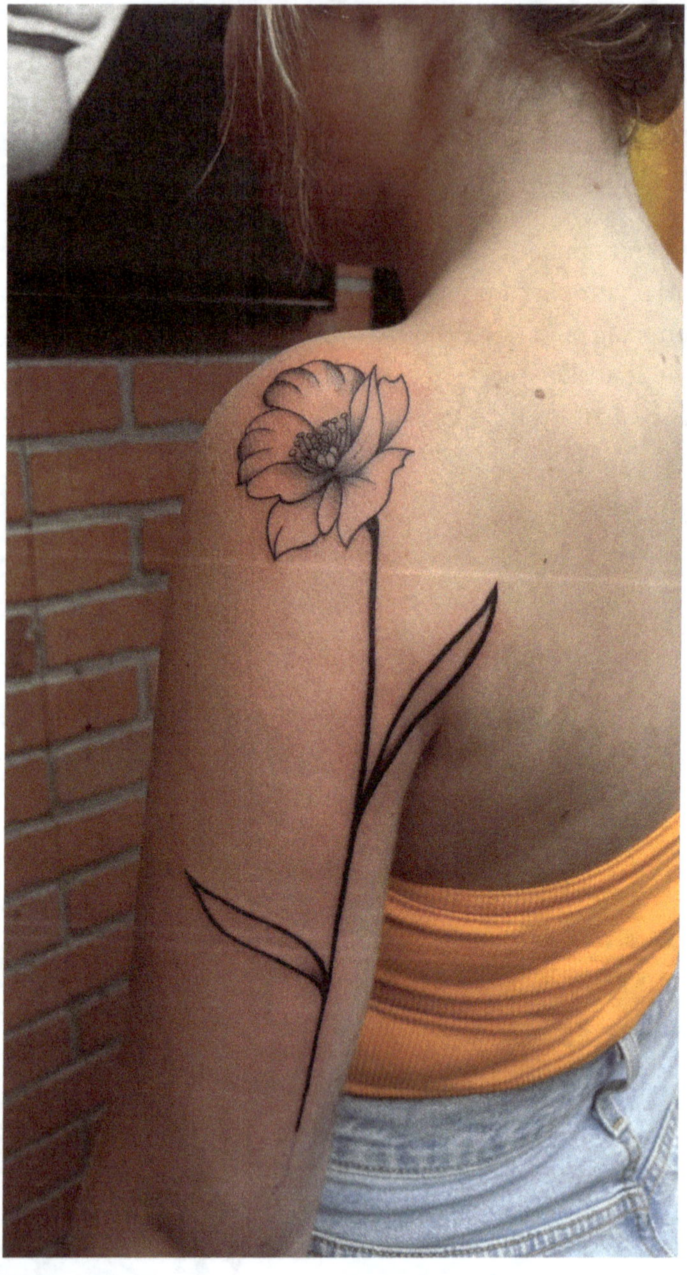

As many of you know, grief comes in waves. Ride them. Cry, be sad, confused, angry, just ride the waves. Let them take you where you need to go and show you how you need to heal. Try to find closure; it is never going to make losing a loved one okay, but remember they are always with you, holding your hand while you ride those waves.

Many life lessons need to be unpacked here. Being as young as I was when I lost my Popi, I did not have the coping skills an adult may have. I didn't know how to express my feelings, which changed my perspective on relationships. I was scared to get close to people because, after experiencing the painful loss of a family member, I realized people could be gone in an instant. That was a whole new scary ballgame for me. What I have come to realize as an adult is you can't let fear hold you back, especially in relationships with loved ones. You may never reach the full potential of the relationship and could be missing out on so many different life lessons and wisdom.

Yes, I am still deeply afraid of losing the people I love, but living in that fear will not benefit anyone, especially myself. God does not want us to live in fear. 1 John 4:18 says, "There is no fear in love, but perfect love casts out fear. For fear has to do with punishment, and whoever fears has not been perfected in love" (ESV).

This verse encourages me to build relationships grounded in a love so pure that it dismantles any fear within a relationship. I still have a fear of losing people, but I try my hardest not to let it get in the way of the potential for all my relationships. I remember that God's love is perfect. It removes any reason for fear in my relationship with Him, and with God's perfect love by my side, I can learn to love and be loved.

The grief of losing my Popi brought me closer to my dad. Although this lesson came about 13 years later, I have a greater understanding of my father and am blessed to share this connection with him as an adult. I realized that everyone experiences grief differently, but it is a generational experience.

Knowing how this loss affected his not being able to have a new adult relationship with his father gave me a deeper understanding of who my dad is as a person. My dad always puts on a strong front and has always been strong for our family. He has always taken care of us and sacrificed so much.

I know my dad is strong, but opening up to me about the loss of his father showed me the sensitive side of him, and honestly, I needed to see that. I needed to see the vulnerability to know that it is okay for me to be vulnerable around him too. This has shown me that loss can be a changing process that is shared with family. It is not an individual process, but a journey that we navigate alongside family. Loss, as hard as it is, becomes a path where we learn, adapt, and find meaningful ways to honor those we miss so dearly, strengthening our relationships as we move forward as a family.

Over time, you will come to understand loss differently. I carry the memories of my Popi as a source of strength. You will find peace or closure one day, and that will look different for everyone. You will learn to live with the pain in a way that honors your lost loved one, and you will become stronger than you ever thought was possible.

Moments of Reflection

Take the time to write to your younger self and comfort them through the loss of someone you love deeply. Your younger self could be when you were a child, like me, or maybe you were in your 30s or 40s. It does not matter how old you were when you experienced this grief that is coming to your mind. Write to your younger self and comfort and guide them through the waves of grief.

_____

_____

_____

_____

_____

_____

_____

_____

_____

_____

_____

_____

_____

_____

_____

_____

_____

Breathe in, Breathe Out, and Smell the Lavender

I didn't realize how much grief and loss I would experience, especially in such a short amount of time and at only 21 years old. My mom's mom, whom I simply called Grandma, passed away when I was 16. She and I were close, and she had an extraordinary relationship with God.

I have had amazing, memorable encounters with family members right before they got sick or passed away. I am not sure why, but I have always seen everyone I have lost in a beautiful light before things went downhill.

This was especially true for my grandmother. I remember she came up for my 16th birthday. Everything was great, and it was a milestone birthday, so it was really special to spend it with close family. She was completely fine until about a month later, when she unexpectedly collapsed.

Like my Popi, she was young as well. She had beaten cancer before, but it came back more aggressively than ever. After my 16th birthday, we found out the cancer was stage four, and her inevitable fate was before her. She was a fighter and did everything right, but God wanted to take her to paradise instead.

Although it was hard for me, she certainly wasn't afraid to die, because she knew where she was going. I remember the funeral; my mom chose to have lavender and the color purple represented at her celebration of life. The name lavender originates from the Latin root *lavare*, meaning "to wash." I relate this to the Lord: As he washes our sins, he gives us hope and reminds us he is our protector, and he brings peace.

At my Grandma's funeral, you could feel the serenity and peace. The lavender was a great reminder of God's gift to us. My mom also chose lavender because purple is the universal color for cancer, and we prayed over all who are suffering with this terrible disease and dedicated her memorial fund to further cancer research.

My grandmother has helped shape my spiritual beliefs. She influenced my mom spiritually, and my mom has helped me connect with God. When I was with my grandmother, it felt like angels were always around me. She was a walking angel, and I connected spiritual symbols to her.

My last ketamine session had ended with me falling into a lavender field. As I entered this new session, I was curious to see if I would return to the lavender and see my grandmother. When she passed, I was going through a lot healthwise myself and did not get to spend as much time with her as I would have liked due to my own illness battles.

As the medicine entered my veins, I could smell the crisp, sweet lavender smell, and felt the purification and calming effects take over my body. I knew God was giving me a vision blessing, and through God, Grandma came to say hello and had a message for me.

This was a healing message for my mental health journey. There was a lot of lavender and butterflies, which signified my grandmother. However, the imagery that God allowed me to see in this session was spectacular. My Grandma and I were butterflies, flying into the most beautiful, bright white light and then falling back into the lavender. It was like a kid's ride, but incredibly special to me because I could feel her presence in the room as I worked with the medicine. Butterflies symbolize to my mom and me suffering, perseverance, and, ultimately, freedom and beauty. Lavender symbolizes the calming effects of protection, healing, and tranquility.

The one thing I will never forget about this ketamine journey is the feeling I felt as I started to come back to reality from my guided imagery and medicine. I could feel one of those good old grandmother hugs. My grandma had a very distinct way of hugging. They were always super tight, strong, and loving, and there was a lot of back-patting and rubbing during it. I could feel the exact feeling right after the medicine left my system.

I will never forget that feeling. It was feeling the presence of someone I had lost that I loved so dearly. My therapist said I had the biggest smile on my face after that. I definitely needed that hug. I thank God for this visual blessing. He is watching over me and allowing me to feel that hug and to remember my Grandma, the person he chose for me on earth to love and cherish me. Although she is walking with him now, I need to continue to lean on him and surrender my will to Him.

My Grandma always said that I was going to do great and special things. As I've mentioned before, many people have told me that, but I've always wondered how they knew. My grandma was very in touch with God and said that, no matter what, I need to keep fighting because there is a big plan for me.

The Devil doesn't like it because I am saved and continue to spread the truth. He is going to try to take it all away. As it says in John 10:10, "The thief comes only to steal and kill and destroy." But God says in the same verse, "I came that they may have life and have it abundantly." I am confident now that there is a plan for me, or I would not have endured all of this pain and suffering over the years. I am meant to make an impact and a difference that will benefit others.

God does answer our prayers, sometimes not exactly as we intended or expected, but in a better way. With my grandmother, we prayed for the healing of her cancer and healing in general. What was unexpected from this prayer was the abundance of family healing received.

We may not always understand it, and it is a little sad to think about, but losing a loved one can bring people closer together. "God works all things for the good." One of my grandmother's sisters did not talk to her for many years prior to her diagnosis. This was devastating to her.

When my grandma got sick, they decided to put their differences aside and come together to help. They talked, they laughed, they listened to understand each other, forgave each other, and chose love. Even since the passing, the entire family has restored that relationship that we missed so much for years. The family was restored, and that gave my grandmother peace before she passed.

I wish I could have seen and spent more time with my grandmother before she passed. Relationships are the most important thing in this life. You never know the last time you are going to see a loved one. I was lucky enough that she was able to make it out to my sixteenth birthday, and I was able to see her in her happy God life form before she got sick.

As I drifted into the lavender field during the session, I felt enveloped by a warmth that extended beyond mere physical sensation. I felt peace, acceptance, and love that felt almost sacred. This experience taught me that healing isn't just about fixing what's broken or easing pain; it's also about reconnecting with memories, people, and blessings that bring comfort and strength.

The lavender was not only soothing, but it also felt like a portal to my grandmother's presence. In that moment, I realized that healing could also mean feeling accompanied, understood, and seen by something greater than myself, even if it's not physically there.

The lavender didn't erase the grief or sadness, but allowed me to sit with those feelings in a new way. It redefined healing as something gentle and nurturing. I learned that healing could be about holding space for both the hurt and the love and allowing myself to feel the depth of my grief while also feeling the soothing lavender presence.

This experience also reinforced my belief in the importance of nature's beauty (lavender and butterflies) in the healing process. The scent of lavender has since become more than a reminder of my grandmother; it has become a touchstone for me to return to whenever I need grounding or reassurance.

Knowing that I can access this memory and this feeling whenever I encounter lavender brings a sense of happiness and stability, even in the midst of my caustic life. It's a reminder that healing is ongoing, and I can carry pieces of those I've lost within me, finding comfort in the small beauty of nature and under the wings of the Lord.

There is power in symbolic connections. Every time I see the color purple, a lavender field, or butterflies, I always connect it back to my grandmother. It is almost like she is saying hello to me, wanting me to know she is there. My journey was filled with so many spiritual connections that I knew my grandmother was in the room with me the whole time. That is a truly special feeling.

Healing this way through the ketamine and imagery therapy was different from the healing I experienced seeing my Popi. The experience with lavender completely changed my view of healing. Ultimately, this ketamine session with lavender didn't just change how I think about healing; it deepened my understanding that healing is a holistic experience, intertwined by sensory connections, memories, and the willingness to let go of control and surrender to the process, which is very difficult for me to do.

Healing is not always a straight line; sometimes, it's about wandering through a field of lavender, breathing in deeply, and trusting that you're exactly where you're supposed to be, surrounded by the love and guidance of those who came before and the higher being that keeps you now.

From my ketamine experience, I now know that I am being watched over, and Grandma's earthly prayers are being answered as God allows me to witness amazing opportunities to make a true impact in this life. I will always remember her hug, the warm, fuzzy feeling all over my body, and the smell of lavender from inviting her in to work with the medicine with me. Breathe in, breathe out; everything is going to be okay.

Moments of Reflection

Think of a time when you found healing through something symbolic. What is your symbol? Is the symbol something that you connect to someone or a memory? How is this helpful for you? Does it give you peace, or does it bring back memories of trauma? If it brings back memories of trauma, how can you turn this symbol into a positive experience?

_____

_____

_____

_____

_____

_____

_____

_____

_____

_____

_____

_____

_____

_____

_____

_____

_____

_____

Healthy or Not: The Importance of Advocating for Yourself

*A*s a child, I was pretty healthy and active … until I was 12, then things took an unexpected turn, leaving me with severe medical issues. It came out of nowhere, and I was physically debilitated. I couldn't walk, I was in so much pain all the time, my skin was discolored and swollen, and so much more.

My whole life came to a halt. Everything I loved to do, I couldn't do anymore. I wasn't even able to go to school. Doctor after doctor, test after test, with no answers. Every test that doctors thought to run came back normal or normal enough that it would not cause these specific symptoms.

My family and I never gave up; we were going to find an answer, but all of my symptoms were so strange. We consulted with many different specialists, and none of them seemed to be able to figure it out.

After about two years, doctors started saying I was making up these symptoms and that I was faking being sick. Doctors were telling me everything was in my head.

I was so hurt. I couldn't believe the people that I was trusting with my life would think I was purposefully making myself sick or faking it. It made no sense. The visible symptoms I had were impossible to make up, but everything else I was explaining they thought was fake. Not being believed by someone who has so much power over you in life-or-death situations was very dehumanizing for me.

I began to distrust doctors and not go because I did not want to get bashed over and over again. To be honest, I wanted it all to be over. I couldn't deal with the pain anymore, and I remember that being my first suicidal ideation. These feelings were so intense that I did not know how to deal with them, especially at 13 years old.

I was not the young, healthy, happy Mya I once was. I had had enough of doctors telling me everything was in my head just because they were out of ideas or could not find the root of the problem. I was tired, no, exhausted, mentally and physically, and knew there needed to be a different course of treatment.

Even though I felt trapped and at rock bottom, I knew I could not sit around anymore waiting for an answer. I needed God's help to find the strength to stick up for myself to people who had the overall say or "power" over my health at the time. I believe God gave me the courage and push that I needed because I was finally ready to advocate for myself, even to those who have more power than I do.

The first time I truly stuck up for myself was when my mom dragged me to a doctor's appointment after I had wanted so badly to give up. The doctor started talking about changing medication and trying some antidepressants to treat my symptoms, and on and on and on. I stood up and said, "I am sick and tired of doctors treating my symptoms and not the actual problem." I walked right out of that doctor's office with my mom behind me. We got to the car, and both of us broke down in tears. We prayed for answers; we didn't know what to do anymore. It felt like there was no hope, but I knew my mom would not give up.

Later that day, my mom went to a conference for work. She talked to a bunch of people about the situation, and God put an amazing person in her hands. It was another doctor, but this doctor took a different approach and actually listened to try to get to the root of the problem. He was an M.D., but also took a holistic approach. When my mom told me about this, I was initially skeptical, but it seemed like the only option left. As much as I didn't want to go, I went, and let me tell you, I am so thankful I did.

I did not want to try something else because I was overall drained, and I had not heard much about holistic approaches in medicine. There are a lot of people who do not believe in it, but God put this specific doctor in my life for a reason, and somehow, subconsciously, I knew that.

When I arrived at this clinic that practices holistic medicine, it wasn't a traditional doctor's office; everyone was very interactive and knew what to do, regardless of who walked through the door. The staff cared so deeply and had relationships and a connection with their patients. Seeing this different atmosphere was a relief for me because I could feel the warm, welcoming environment and could see how much thought and care went into helping people, just like me, who have been unable to get answers.

I admit I was not the most joyful patient they had. I was in so much pain and at rock bottom, but this clinic never gave up on me. After just one appointment, the doctor came up with some conclusions, one of which was Lyme disease.

In the U.S., most medical professionals are taught to recognize only two strains of Lyme disease, Borrelia burgdorferi and Borrelia mayonii. But the reality is far more complex. Research indicates that there are at least 10 distinct strains of Borrelia capable of causing Lyme disease, many of which are accompanied by other hidden threats, including co-infections such as Babesia, Ehrlichia, Anaplasma, and Bartonella. These co-infections don't just complicate Lyme; they blur the lines between symptoms, often mimicking or masking each other and making diagnosis incredibly difficult.

This complexity is one of the key reasons so many people with Lyme disease go undiagnosed for years. The medical system often isn't equipped to recognize how varied and elusive this illness can be. When patients report symptoms like chronic fatigue, brain fog, joint pain, or neurological issues, they're frequently misdiagnosed, or worse, dismissed altogether. The possibility of Lyme disease, let alone multiple strains and co-infections, often isn't even considered.

Making things even harder, the most common tests, ELISA and Western blot, aren't always reliable. They're designed to detect antibodies, but if the immune system hasn't fully responded yet, or if the strain in question doesn't trigger a strong reaction, those tests can come back falsely negative. This creates a dangerous gap between reality and detection, especially in early stages when treatment can be most effective.

Lyme disease can present like a dozen other illnesses: chronic fatigue syndrome, fibromyalgia, autoimmune conditions, or even psychiatric disorders. And so begins the exhausting cycle: referrals, repeated tests, and vague diagnoses, without real answers.

For me, everything changed when I finally found a doctor who looked beyond the obvious. Someone who listened. Someone who understood that healing starts with being heard. Through a more comprehensive evaluation, we discovered not just Lyme disease but multiple co-infections. That moment, when I finally had a name for what I was experiencing, was life-changing. I went from being dismissed to being believed.

My treatment journey involved an individualized plan that included IV silver and antibiotics, an unconventional mix by some standards, but one that was tailored to my specific case. I was fortunate to find a provider willing to think outside the box and walk beside me every step of the way.

That partnership was more than just medical care; it was the start of a healing process that extended beyond the physical. It gave me hope. It restored my faith in medicine. And it underscored something I now know deeply: advocacy and awareness are essential in the battle against Lyme disease, because so much of it remains hidden in plain sight.

My health journey has been anything but simple. Since a severe case of COVID-19 turned my life upside down, I've been navigating a maze of rare and complex diagnoses: mast cell activation syndrome (MCAS), postural orthostatic tachycardia syndrome (POTS), severe allergies, chronic ovarian cysts, and a genetic blood-clotting disorder. Each condition brought its own set of challenges, but together, they've created a storm that has completely redefined how I live and survive.

MCAS is like living with a ticking time bomb inside me. My body releases mast cells unpredictably, triggering reactions that range from intense nausea to full-blown anaphylaxis. At any given moment, something as small as a scent, a food, or even a temperature change can send my system into chaos. And yet, despite the severity of these episodes, too many ER visits end with blank stares or misinformed judgments. I'm not looking for pity, I'm just asking to be taken seriously when I tell them that this could kill me.

Then there's POTS, which turns something as ordinary as standing up into a battle. My heart races, I get dizzy, I feel like I'm about to collapse. Everyday tasks, such as getting out of bed, showering, and walking across a room, can drain me completely. And yet, POTS is often brushed off as anxiety or "just being out of shape," forcing many of us to fight twice: once against the symptoms, and again to be believed.

Severe allergies add another layer of unpredictability. I've had to use an EpiPen more times than I can count. Even though my specialists insist I seek emergency care after reactions, I'm often met with skepticism. I've been intubated. I've been stabilized. However, I've also been dismissed, leaving me feeling like a problem rather than a patient. It's humiliating. And worse, it's dangerous.

On top of it all, I live with a genetic mutation, MTHFR, that affects how my body processes essential nutrients like folate. This isn't just a line on a lab report; it translates into debilitating fatigue, migraines, and mood instability. Yet many doctors still don't acknowledge its significance, leaving patients like me feeling abandoned by the very system we turn to for help.

The result? Countless ER visits, often weekly. Not because I want to be there, but because my body gives me no choice. Yet each visit chips away at my hope. The sighs. The subtle eye rolls. The way staff speak about me, not to me. Sometimes I leave feeling worse than when I arrived, not physically, but emotionally. Those moments of invalidation have led me to some of my darkest places, where the pain wasn't just physical, but profoundly mental and spiritual too.

We need change. We need more medical education around complex, chronic, and rare conditions. We need doctors who are willing to listen before they judge and ask questions instead of making assumptions. Because better understanding leads to better care, and for patients like me, that difference could be lifesaving.

By telling my story, I hope to offer a voice to the voiceless. To remind healthcare providers that behind every chart is a human being. We are not "frequent flyers," "dramatic," or "overreacting." We are people who desperately want to live, not just survive, and who deserve to be treated with dignity, compassion, and respect.

This journey has tested me in every way imaginable, but it's also made me an advocate for myself and for others who are too exhausted, too afraid, or too unheard to keep fighting alone.

Trying to navigate the American healthcare system often feels like stepping into a labyrinth: confusing, exhausting, and deeply isolating. At the heart of the struggle is the way care is fragmented. Patients are bounced from specialist to specialist, each one focused solely on their corner of the body, rarely stepping back to look at the whole person. Instead of feeling cared for, many patients feel like a collection of disconnected symptoms no one wants to fully understand.

This compartmentalized model creates a dangerous gap: who's actually looking at the full picture? Often, no one. Each specialist spends a few minutes on their narrow slice of expertise, while critical connections between symptoms are missed. Communication between providers is limited, if it happens at all. And the patient is left to play messenger, trying to piece together a diagnosis without the medical degree.

Worse still, when symptoms span multiple systems or defy simple categorization, patients, especially women and those with chronic illnesses, are too often dismissed as "dramatic," "anxious," or "psychosomatic." These careless labels can follow patients in their records, shaping future care before the next doctor even walks into the room. It becomes a cycle: not being believed, not being treated, and not being able to heal.

The emotional cost of this cycle is enormous. You're not just battling your body, you're fighting to be heard. The loneliness, the gaslighting, the exhaustion of explaining your pain over and over again with no resolution, all wear you down. It can make you question yourself. It can make you give up.

I know this because I've lived it. For years, I was sent from one specialist to another, each one more focused on ruling things out than truly understanding what was going on. I was made to feel like a puzzle with missing pieces, as if no one wanted to take on the responsibility of solving it. That changed when I finally found a doctor who saw me as a whole person, not a case number. They listened. They connected the dots. They cared. And for the first time, I felt something powerful: hope.

That experience taught me something life-changing: some-times you have to be your own advocate before anyone else will fight for you. You have to ask the hard questions. You have to push back. You have to keep looking for providers who don't just check boxes but truly listen, who see your symp-toms not as an inconvenience but as clues worth exploring.

In this complex, often broken system, finding a medical team that values collaboration, curiosity, and compassion can change everything. When patients are seen, heard, and believed, real healing can begin, not just physically, but emotionally too.

The path to a diagnosis is rarely straightforward. But with the right people beside you and the courage to keep going, it becomes something more than survival; it becomes empow-erment. And that, ultimately, is what every patient deserves.

Looking back, it is crazy how much the medical system failed me. I am not saying it is all bad, but it definitely has its flaws. Some people have great experiences, but most people I talk to don't. Being dismissed when it comes to your health and your body is something you should not tolerate. Being dismissed over and over makes it harder to advocate for yourself. It can even make you question yourself, but it is important to remember you are strong and can fight for yourself and your best interests, especially when it comes to your health and quality of life.

Because of all this, I have had so much medical trauma over the years. I get extreme anxiety when I have to go to the doctor, or I know something is wrong. This should not be the case, but thankfully, my anxiety around my health got better after this one specific ketamine session.

I was drifting off into the Medicine. Suddenly, my mind went chaotic, but I remained still. I heard ambulance sirens; I even heard the doctor and my therapist at the clinic say, "Call 911." I was in an ambulance being rushed to the hospital because there was a problem with the ketamine; I was having an allergic reaction to it and not breathing. I remained still, my body calm; I did not move.

That didn't actually happen. That was my ketamine journey, and God was telling me that no matter what happens, I am going to be okay and taken care of. The breakthrough point through all of that was that I stayed calm. Even though that was not an actual situation, it felt so real. Since this experience, I have had less anxiety because I know I am going to be more than okay healthwise, even if something does happen.

Even though the medical professionals have all my different diagnoses, they still treat me like I am just doing things for attention. This shouldn't be the case, but unfortunately, it can be. If a doctor cannot find out what is wrong with you, they throw their hands up and blame it on mental health. Most of them tend to give up, and I was fortunate enough to find a team of medical professionals who actually listened to me.

Through all of this, I have learned many life-changing lessons. Self-advocacy is essential. There is definitely a right way and a wrong way to do it, but in my story, I remained calm and respectful. The bottom line is I wanted my core problem treated, not just the symptoms. You know your body, and trusting yourself and your instincts is important. It is essential to be persistent in the face of adversity. I was told so many dehumanizing things, and I kept fighting. I knew something was wrong and was determined to get to the bottom of it.

In my search for health healing, I am so thankful I found doctors over the years who listened with their own ears and looked with their own eyes. They took the time to understand what was wrong and did not give up on me. Not every doctor is like this, but when you find the right one, it is truly a blessing. I would like to thank the doctors who have supported me throughout my journey and never given up on me.

Remember, you are your biggest advocate. You know your body better than anyone else. Always listen to your gut and fight for your health. You deserve to live life to its fullest and not let your health get in the way because someone does not believe something is wrong. Fight for yourself!

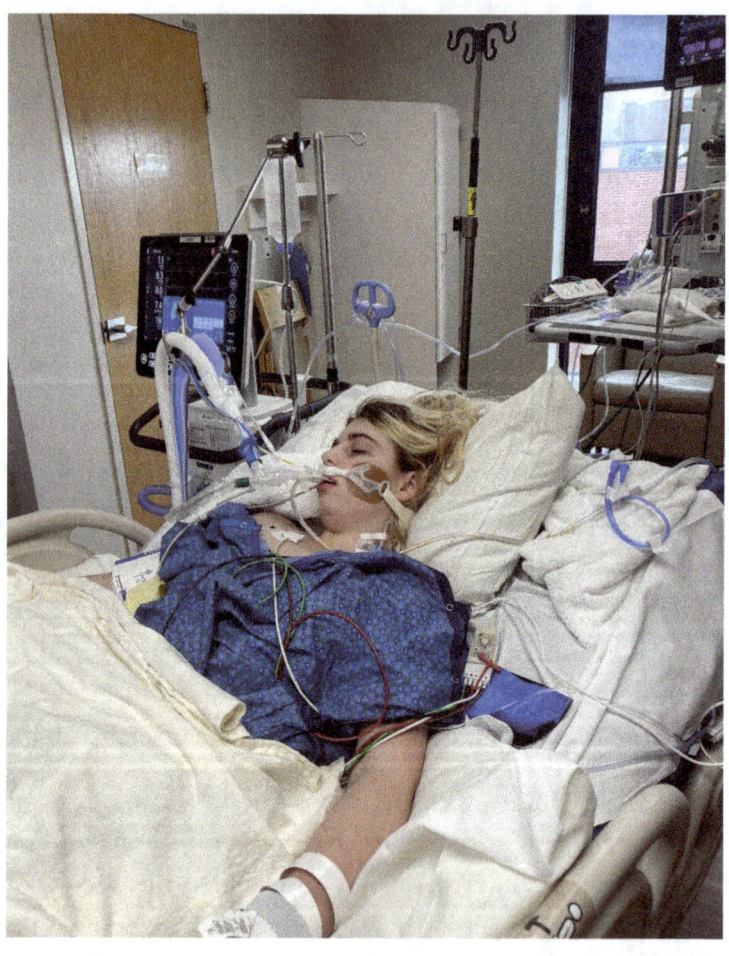

Moments of Reflection

❧ When was the last time you had to advocate for yourself? Was this a positive or negative experience?

_____

_____

_____

_____

_____

_____

❧ Was there a time when you felt misunderstood? Did you advocate for yourself then?

_____

_____

_____

_____

_____

❧ If not, how might things have improved, or how might the outcome have been different?

_____

_____

_____

_____

_____

Who Am I Behind
the Screens?

I grew up in the social media era we are in now, and it has significantly shaped my experiences and perceptions. I have always been fascinated by social media, but over the years, I have wondered who I would be without it. This has left me questioning my identity independent of it. We all get caught mindlessly scrolling, posting the best moments of our life, comparing ourselves to others, but where is the realness within this social media that is so easily accessible with carefully crafted images?

Trust me, I have posted things that make me look like I'm doing great, even when I have been at rock bottom. Sometimes I was even lying in a hospital bed, dealing with my own health issues, and I would post cheerful images when my self-esteem was at its lowest, when I had no motivation, when I was isolating from my friends and family, and when I was caught up in things that seemed so monumental at the time but really weren't. I would still share smiles and positive updates, giving others a glimpse of happiness that masked my inner turmoil. Why did I feel like I had to show the world that my life was perfect when it was really crashing down around me?

Social media became popular when I was young. Everyone had it. People were posting on Instagram, Snapchatting, and so much more. Everyone around my age and younger has grown up behind a screen. It can take away part of your true identity, and you might not know who you are without it.

I think social media can lead to feelings of inadequacy and low self-esteem. This is what I believe has been some of my battles with anxiety and depression. For me, it was always validation. This is hard for me to admit, but it feels nice posting a picture and having people tell me how amazing and pretty I am; that is the validation I am talking about.

The real question is, would you get the same type of engagement if you posted something that wouldn't go on your highlight reel? This leads to a comparison with others. Essentially, basing my self-worth on others' accomplishments or circumstances. This caused me to overlook my own strengths and progress. This has led to dissatisfaction in my life and has even paralyzed my growth.

The pure exhaustion of maintaining this picture-perfect image can be overwhelming. We want people to see when we are living our best life, or make it look like we are living our best life. The struggle between presenting an ideal self and embracing my own feelings was a constant battle. None of us knows how to be completely real on social media all the time. I am not saying that this is always a bad thing. I don't necessarily post the hard things in my life because I may want to keep them private or don't want to bring anyone else down.

What I do wish that I did not do is post something that looks like I am doing amazing, when deep down I am hurting and wrestling with my inner demons. We often use social media as a cover-up. We post what we want people to see or what we want people to think about us.

The realization and reality for me are much deeper. I realized we must prioritize our spiritual identities over our social ones. God doesn't measure us by our popularity or the number of likes we receive; He desires a genuine relationship with us.

It goes so much deeper than that, and the truth is, you need to be consumed by your spiritual identity, not your social identity. I will be honest, I find myself consumed more by my social identity at times. God doesn't care how popular you are or how many likes you get on a post. God wants you to walk with him, enjoy life, and be in the moment. When we are off this path with God, that's when the loneliness, self-comparison, anxiety, and depression start to creep in.

My social identity dominated my spiritual identity, which led to a complete loss of self. The lack of harmony between my outward appearance and inner feelings only deepened the sense of isolation I felt. Despite having a positive platform, I still felt the weight of social norms pushing me to showcase an idealized version of myself.

When I started college, I lost who I was. I was so mad at the world and upset about all the different things that had happened to me. I completely changed what I believed in to fit into the college realm.

I am proud to say this is not the case anymore, but it was hard to pull myself out of that long, twisty, dark road. I faced burn-out from trying to meet all these social expectations and lost sight of who I really was and who I wanted to be.

Struggling between presenting an ideal self and embracing my true feelings was a constant battle. All the shared smiles while feeling broken inside, seeking validation from likes and comments, made me perceive this as being valued and heard.

The more I did this, the more I understood how this habit of showcasing only the good moments was draining me. It trapped me in a cycle of hiding my struggles. It was as if I were creating a mask that I couldn't take off, which pressured me to meet a certain standard of happiness and success that wasn't always real.

The more I maintained this mask, the more disconnected I felt. This realization became a turning point, showing me that true self-worth couldn't be found in external validation but needed to come from within. I wanted people to see the honesty and acceptance of my whole self.

One thing I find to be very true is that we all have idols. Not the idols you may be thinking of, but the things that get in the way of having an authentic relationship with God. It can be appearance, fitness, the people you spend time around, finances, and even yourself. These things can block you from having a true connection and relationship with God.

It's important to identify those idols; for me, sometimes it is social media. I can sit there scrolling and comparing myself to others instead of spending time with God. Find your idols and see what is holding you back from getting a true, loving relationship with God. An idol I have always struggled with is getting too consumed in my social identity. I have had to step back and remember that my relationship with God is so much more important to me than how others may perceive me.

As I began to recognize the emptiness of seeking validation online, I found myself searching for something deeper: my spiritual identity. Unlike the temporary satisfaction of social media approval, my spiritual identity offered a grounding sense of peace and purpose that wasn't dependent on anyone else's opinions. God's love is perfect. He has shown me unconditional love and has proven to me time and time again that I should turn to Him.

When you shift your focus to your spiritual identity, you gain inner peace, resilience, authenticity, and so much more. Spiritual identity allows you to have a deeper sense and understanding of peace and fulfillment independent of society's validation. You become more resilient because spiritual identity is permanent and unchanging. You get a sense of sustainability. You can live more authentically because you are living the life that aligns with your personal values rather than the social norms of the time.

There is a way to balance both identities, and when you do, you feel freer and more true to yourself, giving you a sense of purpose. The first step to having a balance is simply being aware. Be aware when you are only focusing on your social identity and redirect by journaling, reading, and spending time with God every day.

I learned that when I centered myself in my faith, I felt stronger, more resilient, and less susceptible to the highs and lows of online approval. In prayer, quiet reflection, and moments of gratitude, I began to feel whole, reminding myself that my worth was already affirmed by something greater. I would journal and set aside time for myself and time for gratitude. This helped me heal, and this focus helped me see that my spiritual identity wasn't just a part of me; it was my foundation. This foundation offered clarity and strength in a world that often pulls us in conflicting directions. I had to remind myself that my connection to God far outweighs any external perceptions.

Find what works for you. I am not saying completely eliminate your social identity, but make sure you find time for your spiritual identity. It is all about balance. With that balance, you will have a more fulfilling life and a lasting relationship with God.

Moments of Reflection

❧ What are the steps you can take to have a balance between your social and spiritual identity?

_____

_____

_____

_____

_____

_____

❧ Do you feel overwhelmed and consumed by social media?

_____

_____

_____

_____

_____

_____

❧ How can you find a healthy balance and turn to the Lord for affirmation?

_____

_____

_____

_____

_____

Beyond the Game:
The Pressure to Perform

I grew up in a family where athletics weren't just hobbies, they were woven into the rhythm of our lives. My parents both competed at high levels: my mom ran cross-country and track at Colorado State University, and my dad played baseball at the University of Florida until injuries changed his path. Competition, commitment, and grit were part of the language we spoke at home.

My sport was soccer. I tried just about everything growing up, but the soccer field was where my world made the most sense. It was where I learned discipline, joy, belonging, and even heartbreak. It was where my closest friendships formed and where I felt most at home.

Soccer wasn't just something I did; it became the place where I built my identity. Eventually, all the practices, tournaments, and miles traveled led to an offer to play Division I soccer at the University of Northern Colorado. I remember opening that email and feeling a surge of possibility. It felt like confirmation that everything I had sacrificed was finally worth it.

But like every athlete eventually learns, the path isn't linear. Before college and throughout it, injuries became unwanted but persistent companions. Three major knee surgeries on the same knee, interrupted seasons, and reshaped timelines forced me to confront physical limits I never expected to face so young. Torn ACL. Torn meniscus. Cartilage damage. Procedures. Rehab. Repeat.

Injuries are part of sports, but no one prepares you for how deeply they test your mind, not just your body. Sitting on the sidelines during games and practices was often more painful than the surgeries themselves. I desperately wanted to be out there doing what I loved, contributing, competing, being part of the team rhythm. And while my teammates and coaches supported me, I still battled an internal world that felt heavy, loud, and exhausting.

That's where the difference between mental toughness and mental health became painfully clear.

Mental toughness helps you push through grueling work-outs, keeps you going when your legs burn, and helps you stay disciplined when you're exhausted. It's what makes athletes show up with grit and determination. But mental health is what happens when the lights go off, when you're sitting alone with your thoughts, when comparison settles in, when the fear of failure becomes louder than your confidence. Mental toughness builds resilience, but mental health is what determines how you survive the quiet moments that no one else sees.

For me, mental toughness was never the issue. I could push through pain, exhaustion, obstacles, and fear. What I struggled with was the voice in my head that whispered:

What if you're not enough?

What if people notice your mistakes?

What if you come back ... and you're not the same?

I wasn't just afraid of messing up on the field; I was terrified of failing in life. I tied my identity so tightly to being an athlete that any setback felt like a threat to who I was.

But faith has a way of tugging gently on your heart, even when you're convinced you can carry everything on your own. In quiet moments, usually when I was icing my knee alone at night, I felt God reminding me that identity isn't something you earn. It's something already given. He knew me beyond my jersey number, beyond the wins, beyond the setbacks. I didn't fully understand that yet, but the seed was planted.

As the injuries piled up, learning opportunities did too. I began to realize that failure wasn't final, it was formative. Every setback taught me something about myself: how I adapt, how I persevere, how I lean into God when I have nothing left to give. And every success, big or small, reminded me that joy exists alongside pain, not instead of it.

There were incredible moments as an athlete that I still cherish. The thrill of winning rivalry games. The pure rush of scoring a goal. The feeling of knowing I played my best game. The camaraderie of celebrating victories, sweating through conditioning together, and laughing in locker rooms. My teammates in college were not the reason I struggled—they were doing the best they could while fighting their own battles.

Collegiate athletics are demanding, and everyone copes differently. I never blame them for what I was struggling with privately.

Still, when I faced my third major surgery, and this time, complications that required me to be resuscitated, I had to confront a reality bigger than soccer: my life mattered more than the game. My physical and mental health were no longer negotiable. Returning to the field meant risking not only another season but potentially my future.

I remember waking up after that surgery, groggy and shaken, knowing instantly that something in me had shifted. The question became painfully clear: If another injury could put my health or my life on the line, was continuing to play worth everything I was sacrificing?

The answer was no. My body was tired. My mind was tired. And deep down, my spirit was too.

Choosing to retire took a kind of courage I didn't know I had. People assume quitting is a weakness, but walking away from something that shaped your entire identity requires more resilience, not less. I wasn't giving up, I was choosing to live. I was choosing peace. I was choosing to trust that God had more for me than the identity I was clinging to.

But the questions that followed were overwhelming:

Who am I without soccer?

Who am I without that label, that recognition, that role?

How will I afford school?

What else do I love?

What else am I even good at?

These questions haunted me more than any defender or running drill ever could.

During this time, my faith became both a lifeline and a learning curve. I believed in God, but I didn't always know how to trust Him with the parts of my identity I had white-knuckled for so long. It was easier to trust Him with my future than with the pieces of myself I wasn't ready to let go of.

Identity had to be rebuilt brick by brick, and faith became the foundation of that rebuilding. When I didn't know who I was, God reminded me who He created me to be. When I felt lost, He whispered hope. When I felt alone, He placed people and opportunities in my path that proved I wasn't.

I also realized that college environments, like any community, have both strengths and limitations. The University of Northern Colorado offered me opportunities, experiences, and lessons I'll always be grateful for. My decision to leave was not a judgment on the school or the program; it was a recognition of what I personally needed during an incredibly vulnerable season of my life. Sometimes environments are good, but not the right fit. Sometimes people are kind but unable to fully understand what you're going through. That doesn't make them bad; it just means your journey is calling you elsewhere.

Leaving soccer meant leaving UNC, and that was one of the most difficult decisions I ever made. Walking away in the middle of my academic career felt terrifying. But deep down, I knew I needed a fresh start, a place where an injury timeline or a roster position didn't define me. A place where I could rediscover life beyond the sport that had shaped so much of me.

The lesson I carry now is simple but powerful: Your sport does not define you. Your identity is not limited to a role, a jersey, or a talent. You are capable of more than you ever imagined.

And God has a way of leading us into chapters we never saw coming, especially when the ones we clung to begin to close.

Looking back now, I see how God used every injury, every doubt, every lonely moment, and every tear-stained night to guide me toward a life that is fuller, steadier, and more rooted than the one I was desperately trying to hold onto. I didn't lose myself when I left soccer; I found the parts of me I never knew existed. And if you're reading this, maybe this is your reminder that endings are often just disguised beginnings. You are allowed to choose a new path. You are allowed to protect your peace. And you are allowed, always, to trust that God is leading you somewhere good.

Moments of Reflection

Reflect on a time when there was a lot of pressure for you to perform extremely well on something. It could be a sport, a project, or an activity—anything that comes with a lot of pressure. How did this pressure affect you mentally? Did it affect you physically?

_____

_____

_____

_____

_____

_____

_____

_____

_____

_____

_____

_____

_____

_____

_____

_____

_____

_____

_____

Breaking the Silence

*W*hat I am going to discuss next may be very triggering and could be difficult for some readers. If you become triggered or feel overwhelmed, please feel free to skip this chapter.

Right after my 18th birthday, I was sexually assaulted by a man I was just getting to know. I ended up having to go to the hospital, get everything checked out, and make sure there weren't going to be any long-lasting injuries.

For a very long time, I carried immense guilt and shame about what had happened. I continuously questioned whether it was my fault, wondering whether I should not have gone on a date with this guy. I replayed the scenario in my mind, searching for different choices I could have made.

Working through the guilt and shame, I realized that a lot of survivors deal with the same emotions after being sexually assaulted. We live in a society where people immediately ask, "What were you wearing?" "Were you drinking?" or simply just say that you were asking for it. I want to emphasize that it does not matter what you were wearing or if you were intoxicated; no one deserves to be violated.

I had just graduated from high school and was going into my freshman year of college. I had heard horror stories of women being sexually assaulted, but I never thought it would happen to me, especially during a seemingly innocent dinner with someone I would be attending college with in a few weeks. The shock and trauma left me feeling lost and isolated; I was ashamed and embarrassed. The experience had taken a part of me, complicating my transition to college life.

This trauma caused me to have unimaginable nightmares, flashbacks, and anxiety that eventually led to a diagnosis of post-traumatic stress disorder (PTSD). I confided in trusted friends and my parents, but advocating for myself and seeking justice was far more complex than simply sharing my story. Many people doubted my experience; they simply could not believe that he would do something like that, or thought I was seeking attention. That added further trauma to my life. I didn't want to go on with life anymore, and at that point, I wished I had kept silent.

So many survivors do not find justice; the legal system is incredibly challenging for women, often discrediting their experiences. I consciously choose to identify as a survivor rather than a victim. While I was in therapy processing all this trauma, I came to realize, with the help of my therapist, that I AM a survivor. I am a survivor of a truly terrible thing that I wouldn't wish upon anyone.

Just weeks after the assault, I began my freshman year. As I mentioned, I was a soccer player at the University of Northern Colorado, and all the athletes at the school had to arrive early in preparation for the upcoming season. What made this even more difficult for me is that the man who sexually assaulted me was also on the football team. His presence on campus, whether in the dining hall or weight room, made me feel trapped, as if I couldn't escape the situation.

Despite my efforts to move forward with my life, I fell into a deep depression, losing significant memories from that part of my freshman year. I felt unheard and defeated, despite having friends who I thought would support me.

My freshman year soccer season ended early for me when I got a stress fracture in my tibia and two unexpected blood clots. Blood clots are pretty unheard of in someone so young, but I had two in my leg and was back on the sideline. This deepened my depression and led to suicidal thoughts. My parents intervened, and I took the second semester of my freshman year off to focus on my mental health and confront my PTSD.

I tried various inpatient facilities, but nothing seemed to help. I found myself making poor choices and associating with the wrong crowd, all while trying to escape my pain through fleeting moments of pleasure. This behavior is not uncommon among survivors like me; many struggle to find a way to cope.

It wasn't until I underwent ketamine therapy that I truly began to process my trauma. It took over two years to reach a point of healing where my PTSD was manageable. During one of my first ketamine sessions, I experienced a profound journey. I remember walking into my session, having journaled that morning, and writing to have no expectations, but great expectations. It was the motto for all of my ketamine journeys.

When I was in the medicine, I began in a dark, unsettling room, reminiscent of the space I was assaulted in, which made me very uncomfortable and fearful; I felt like I had no control.

I started falling out of the room down this dark, deep, what seemed like a never-ending hole. Suddenly, I landed in this beautifully decorated apartment, all pink, blue, and white, exactly the way I wanted to decorate my senior year college apartment. It was bright, welcoming, and beautiful. Everything was okay; I was finally safe.

While this may not seem like a conventional breakthrough, it marked a significant moment in my life. For me, for the first time since the assault, I felt a sense of safety after confronting a painful memory. The ketamine allowed me to reframe that tragic event in my life with a new room, a new beginning filled with hope and brightness.

The last thing I want to say is that even though I might not have achieved the justice I sought, speaking my truth was vital for my healing. It demonstrated my strength and courage. Your story is important, and sharing it matters. Your voice carries weight, and it's important to let it be heard.

Moments of Reflection

❧ Have you ever found yourself in a situation where you needed to speak up?

_____

_____

_____

_____

_____

❧ What was the situation?

_____

_____

_____

_____

❧ How did you feel after speaking up?

_____

_____

_____

_____

❧ What was the outcome?

_____

_____

_____

_____

Grieving the Living:
The People Who Left,
But a God Who Stayed

I 've struggled with how to write this chapter, not because the story isn't clear, but because the emotions have never stopped echoing. I didn't want this to be a "revenge" chapter or a way to call anyone out. I wanted it to be honest. Real. About loss. About friendship. About healing. And most of all, about grace.

It just so happens that as I was trying to find the words to write this chapter, I went to a Bible Study, and the topic of friendship came up. It was there that the breakthrough finally came: we don't just grieve people who pass away. We grieve those who are still alive, those who used to be part of our daily lives but no longer are. That grief is different. It's confusing and open-ended. It comes with silence, not closure.

I think of the friends I've lost, and my heart still aches. Some of those friendships faded slowly, and some ended in a single moment, so fast, so sharp, it left me breathless. And in that grief, I've had to wrestle with the truth that some doors close without explanation. That hurts more than I can describe.

One of the deepest losses was a friend I had known since middle school, someone I truly believed would walk with me through anything. After my sexual assault, I was already fragile and trying to pull myself back together. I had stepped away from school to breathe, to heal, to simply survive. During that time, I confided in her, hoping for comfort and understanding.

Instead, she casually mentioned that she was going on a ski trip with a group of friends... a group that included him, the man who assaulted me.

She explained that the trip had been paid for, almost as if she needed me to understand the practical side of it. But practicality didn't soften the blow. I remember sitting there in disbelief, listening as if she were giving me an ordinary update, as if this wasn't deeply connected to my pain. As if the presence of the person who traumatized me was just a small detail.

It wasn't just the trip. It was the message underneath it: he mattered more. The trip mattered more. And in that moment, it was as if my pain was invisible.

That friendship had to end. The door had to close. Because it was a choice between holding on to someone who minimized my trauma or choosing myself. And choosing myself felt like tearing off a limb.

But I wasn't perfect, either. I want to be honest about that. I wasn't the best version of myself in those years. I made a lot of bad decisions out of pain, confusion, and desperation. I self-sabotaged constantly. I pushed people away even as I begged them to stay. I lashed out. I isolated. I made it hard for people to walk with me.

And still, I needed them. I needed grace. But instead of growing stronger together, many of those friendships withered under the weight of my chaos. I get it, well, I get it as much as I can. I know I was hard to be around. But it doesn't make the loss any easier.

It's hard when people judge you by the lowest season of your life. When they only see the broken version and decide that's who you are. When your whole existence gets reduced to a moment, a mistake, or a breakdown they witnessed, and that becomes their conclusion about your worth. It's a painful kind of judgment. Because none of us is just one moment. None of us is just the mistakes we made when we were trying to survive.

And I was trying so desperately to survive. I still felt misunderstood, even dismissed. The pressure to be okay, to explain or prove my pain, was crushing.

On top of everything, there was my anxiety. The instability. The spiraling. I felt like a burden. Like a warning sign no one wanted to stop for. That is its own kind of pain, being judged not just for your decisions, but for the very battles you didn't ask to fight.

That's the grief I've carried, not just for the people who left, but for the why. The unanswered questions. The wondering if it was all my fault. I know I was a mess. I own that. But I still ask: "Why didn't they stay? Why didn't they try to understand? Why did they give up on me?"

Grieving people who are still alive is its own kind of heartbreak. Especially when you don't get clarity, when the "why" goes unanswered, when you know you were messy, hurting, difficult, but still hoped someone would stay.

I've asked God a thousand times why people left me. Why did they close the door and never look back? Sometimes, I still don't know the answer. But I do know this: God never walked away, even when I was a mess. Even when I couldn't love myself. Even when I made choices I regret. And maybe that's the lesson that keeps unfolding, not that we'll always get closure, but that healing isn't about them coming back. It's about learning to stay with yourself and letting God stay with you too.

Through Bible study, I've been challenged to ask what kind of friend God would want me to be. Romans 12:10 tells us to be devoted to one another in love, to honor others above ourselves. That verse weighs heavily on my heart. Because it reminds me that true friendship isn't about perfection, it's about presence. About grace. About choosing people even when they're not easy to love.

I didn't have a ketamine journey tied to this pain. But I've had a deeply spiritual one. A journey through abandonment, trauma, mental breakdown, and isolation. And somehow, God has met me in every layer of that darkness.

I'm still healing. I'm still learning. Still letting go. But I've come to see that some friendships were only meant for a season, and some losses hold lessons too deep to ignore.

So I'll leave you with this: Have you ever let someone else's judgment of you, someone's decision to leave, or a single bad moment, become the story you tell yourself about who you are?

Because I have, and it almost destroyed me.

But what I'm learning, what I have to keep learning, is that I am not defined by who left.

I am not the sum of my lowest moment.

I am not just the version of myself someone saw when I was barely surviving.

And neither are you.

We are becoming. We are healing. And we are still here.

There's something sacred about the people who stay. But there's also something holy about the God who stays, even when no one else does.

So if you're grieving someone who's still alive ...

If you're still holding on to unanswered questions, still aching for someone to understand, still wondering why they walked away ...

Know this:

You don't need their permission to heal.

You don't need their understanding to be whole.

You don't need to carry the shame of being judged in a glimpse of time.

God knows the full picture. He sees the whole story. And He stayed.

Let this be the season where you stop chasing those who couldn't carry your pain and start trusting the One who already carried you.

You are not too much.

You are not too broken.

You are not unseen.

You are loved. You are being healed. You are being held.

And the story isn't over.

Moments of Reflection

❧ Have you ever been betrayed by someone you thought you could trust?

_____

_____

_____

_____

_____

_____

_____

_____

❧ What emotions come up when you think about this betrayal?

_____

_____

_____

_____

_____

_____

_____

_____

_____

Hotty Toddy:
An Unexpected Destination

When I decided to leave the University of Northern Colorado, I sensed there was something greater awaiting me, a place where I could discover my purpose outside of soccer. I have always loved the South; my mom often believed that I was destined to live there.

Spoiler alert: I ended up at Ole Miss (The University of Mississippi) halfway through my sophomore year of college. It is funny how I ended up there. This story beautifully illustrates how God always has a plan for each of us.

In November 2022, I confided in my parents about my desire to transfer for the next semester. I felt strongly that I couldn't go another year at the University of Northern Colorado; it simply wasn't the right fit for me. As applications to transfer were due that month, I applied to several southern schools, with the University of Kentucky being one of my top picks.

Accompanied by my mom, I toured the University of Kentucky, but something just felt off. I didn't feel at peace; it just didn't resonate with me. After the tour, I found myself in tears, uncertain about what to do next, when suddenly, I received a text that would change everything.

"Hotty Toddy, Mya!" was the opening line of the message. My immediate thought was, *What the heck is Hotty Toddy?* Spoiler alert: it doesn't have a specific meaning. But at Ole Miss, it is a saying, a sense of community, a term of endearment, a hello, or a shout-out in a sports game. It's special, although it doesn't mean much. Yet, to me, it carried immense significance. The rest of the text read, "Congratulations, you have been accepted into Ole Miss!"

I was taken aback, as I had applied to Ole Miss on a whim, following a recommendation from my dad, not having much knowledge of the school. This text arrived while I was still in Kentucky, and the last orientation day for Ole Miss transfer students was that Saturday, only a day and a half away. Initially, my mom was against the seven-hour drive for the orientation and missing a few more days of work.

Despite her initial reluctance, she eventually agreed to go, and her story is quite remarkable. As we drove to Oxford, Mississippi, I felt a joy that my mom had never seen in me before. The downtown area of Oxford, known as the Square, was beautifully decorated for Christmas, and as we cruised through at the beginning of December, I was struck by its stunning beauty. A wave of comfort washed over me, and I felt an overwhelming sense of peace, even before the tour.

The next morning, my mom and I attended the Ole Miss transfer student orientation and tour. The campus was gorgeous; it was everything I loved about the South. Throughout my time there, I couldn't stop smiling and felt an infectious excitement. By the end of the tour, I accepted my admission and prepared to start classes just weeks later.

Curious about my mom's earlier hesitation, I asked her, "Why were you so hesitant to come for this tour? What changed your mind?" She burst into laughter and replied, "I stubbed my toe." I was baffled by this response, but I listened as she elaborated. At that moment, I understood how deeply God was watching over me and had a plan in motion.

As I have mentioned, my mom has an amazing relationship with God, one that I hope to form with Him as well. She explained that when I told her and my dad that I wanted to transfer, she prayed, and God communicated to her, "It's going to happen, and it's going to happen fast, so be ready to act."

She described how she was praying in Kentucky, seeking discernment, and heard that phrase again. Feeling frustrated and uncertain, she accidentally stubbed her toe as she walked. This moment forced her to pause, sit down, and reflect on the "Hotty Toddy" email and the drive to Mississippi. It was a swift revelation of God's purpose for me. Everything fell into place for her, and she realized I was meant to go on this tour at Ole Miss, which was conveniently within driving distance.

Though initially puzzled by God's message, once she arrived in Oxford, she felt a profound sense of peace, recognizing that this was where I was destined to complete my college journey and embark on a new chapter. God knew this all along and ensured I arrived there, even if it required a bit of persuasion and faith. He has never failed me, and I trust that He is the guiding light in my life.

You never know where life will lead you. I had no clue where I was meant to finish my college experience. I applied to Ole

Miss because my dad mentioned it has a really pretty campus and thought I might enjoy it, but I wasn't familiar with the school. Ultimately, I found my way there because it was God's plan, and I have learned and achieved so much on my path to healing and discovering my purpose.

Moments of Reflection

❧ Have you ever had an unexpected destination that turned out to be the best for you?

_____

_____

_____

_____

_____

_____

❧ What was your destination, and what were the unintentional and intentional steps that led you there?

_____

_____

_____

_____

_____

_____

❧ Did it change your life? If so, in what way?

_____

_____

_____

_____

_____

_____

A New Journey:
Finding My Purpose

*W*hen I decided to leave the University of Northern Colorado, I knew there was more for me out there. A better place for me to find my true purpose. My parents struggled with my leaving my former school right in the middle of the year and wanting to move halfway across the country. As I said, God told my mom, "It's going to happen really fast, and you will just know."

Taking a leap of faith and going somewhere where I knew absolutely nobody was one of the best decisions of my life, but doing good isn't always black and white, and those shades of gray can be unsettling. Personally, I think things went so poorly in Colorado because I was destined to be at Ole Miss. Sometimes, unexpected experiences can lead us in a new and better direction.

I wasn't a soccer player anymore, but I knew I needed to find something else to get involved in. I became a founding member of the sorority Alpha Chi Omega Lambda Pi chapter and served on the executive board. I met a lot of people and was able to get as involved as I could at Ole Miss. I ended up randomly matching roommates and got some of the best roommates ever; no horror stories there.

Things seemed to be going great until my mental health started to deteriorate. At that point, I was not doing everything I could to help myself. I still was not on my medication consistently and did not go to therapy regularly. This just goes to show that no matter where you go, you still have to put in the work for yourself; you can't run away from your problems.

It took about a year at Ole Miss, which was still an amazing year overall with friends and people, before I decided to face myself and heal. I wouldn't have come to this conclusion if I had not been at Ole Miss. I wanted to be the best version of myself. That is when I discovered ketamine therapy and decided to take a semester off to go home and focus on myself so I could make the most of the amazing experiences that were offered at Ole Miss.

What kick-started me into finding my purpose was a speech I gave to my sorority about mental health and suicide prevention. I gave this speech and left my sisters crying because everyone could understand on a deeper level everything I struggled with.

I was told I am an inspiration. I got texts and social media messages and had face-to-face conversations. I honestly changed some people's lives. That is when I found my true purpose. I knew there was a purpose for me in this world, and without coming to Ole Miss, I am not sure if I would have found it when I did.

I could go on and on about the amazing things offered at Ole Miss, but I will stick to the experiences that helped me. Joining a sorority was a great way for me to make friends, but I ended up withdrawing in the summer of 2024 to focus on other things that I thought would help my mental health.

Being a part of the New Media and Journalism program has helped me discover how much I enjoy writing. The clubs on campus I am a part of, such as Delight Ministries, have helped me grow my faith in a way I did not think was possible. Finally, having those true friends by my side has been a game-changer: friends who check in on me, friends who are rooting for me, and friends who would drop everything when needed.

Coming to Ole Miss wasn't always sunshine and butterflies, but I have accomplished a lot since I have been here. I am a better and happier person. If I had not taken the time to focus on myself, I would probably still be very unhappy, even at Ole Miss. The school opened my eyes and made me want to be the best version of myself possible, and I do not think I would have been able to do that if I were still at the University of Northern Colorado. It was essential to me that I took that leap of faith.

Look at me now! I graduated from Ole Miss with a Bachelor of Science in Integrated Marketing Communications and a minor in Business. I am going to continue writing, and I am ready to go where the world and God take me! This school has supported my dreams and has done everything it could to make them come true.

Sometimes, you have to take a leap of faith to see what is out there for you. The world is waiting. It can be a very scary process, but in my story, in the end, it was worth it. I was so proud walking across that stage knowing that "I did it" and the positive impact I had on people here.

Moments of Reflection

&❧ Have you ever had to take a leap of faith? If so, what was it?

_____

_____

_____

_____

&❧ Did you come out a stronger and better person?

_____

_____

_____

_____

&❧ Did it make you happier?

_____

_____

_____

_____

&❧ What was your personal experience?

_____

_____

_____

_____

A Chapter Ends:
Your Journey Awaits

*A*s I embarked on the journey to write this book, I found myself immersed in uncertainty. I did not know what to expect, and wasn't entirely sure of what lay ahead. When you set out to write a book, things happen that give you the ah-ha moments that catch you off guard and reshape your understanding of things that have happened in your life.

I initially envisioned every detail of this book to be flawless; yet as I reflected on my journey, I had to remind myself that striving for perfection is not only unrealistic but also unnecessary. Life in all its intricate beauty and complexity thrives in its imperfections, and it is these very imperfections that make it worthy of exploration.

I hope that by the time you finish reading this book, you will find some measure of healing, whether that be physical, emotional, or spiritual. The act of writing has brought me healing in ways I never anticipated, uncovering wounds within me that I hadn't even recognized until I began to put words to the thought. This process of expression has proven to be profoundly restorative. I envisioned this book as a tool for healing—not only for myself, but for you as well.

Through the many challenges I've faced, I've uncovered some core truths: resilience is vital, hope is what propels us forward, belief in ourselves can be transformative, and above all, faith is what sustains us through life's toughest trials.

These lessons, often hard-won, have endowed me with strength, clarity, and a sense of peace. It is my sincere wish that they resonate with you and offer similar comfort.

Let's acknowledge a fundamental reality: each person's journey is uniquely their own. In this world of shared existence, we must strive to be compassionate toward ourselves and others. You never truly know the battles that someone else is facing, just as there may be times when others cannot fully grasp your struggles. Embrace grace, extend compassion, practice self-love, and above all, never give up.

This book represents not the conclusion of my narrative but merely one chapter—or perhaps a few chapters—of a larger story. There remains an abundance of learning, experiencing, and healing ahead of me. I am deeply proud of the progress I've made so far, and I hope my story inspires you to take on your own healing journey.

Whether that step is small and tentative or bold and decisive, remember that every forward movement is a victory. You are deserving of the effort, the struggle, and the entire journey. Remember, never give up on yourself; you are worthy of new beginnings and the possibilities they bring.

I used to think a story had to have a clear ending. That when the storm passed, or the dream came true, or the diagnosis was survived, that was the final chapter. I now know better. Life isn't about finding a perfect bow to wrap around your pain or your purpose. It's about learning how to live in the tension between who you were and who you're still becoming.

I've survived things I didn't think I'd talk about out loud. I've healed from things I didn't think I'd live through. This isn't the end. It's the turning of a page, because maybe the next chapter isn't in what happened to me but in what I choose to do next.

Things aren't always easy for me. Yes, I wrote a book, but that doesn't mean I don't still wrestle with anxiety and depression. Life gets heavy sometimes. There are days I feel stuck, like I'm spinning on a merry-go-round with no way out. And honestly? That happens more often than I'd like to admit. That makes me human. Things do not just go away overnight. With hard work and balance, you can become the best version of yourself and who you have always wanted to be.

I still have a lot of work to do on myself. We can always work and strive to be the best versions of ourselves possible. I don't have everything figured out; I don't have most things figured out. But what I do know wholeheartedly is that God is with me, and I am determined to make an impact in the world. Until next time, be you and be perfectly imperfect.

Acknowledgments

Thank you to everyone who made this book possible. I am 22 years old and have so much to share.

This book would not have been possible without Jamie and Becky Woodruff.

I owe my whole village a huge thank you for always sticking by my side and never giving up on me, even in my darkest days.

Thank you, Shanda Trofe, for giving me this opportunity to share my story; you have made this possible for me.

About the Author

$\mathcal{M}$ya Johnson is a first-time author from Fort Collins, Colorado. Formerly a student at the University of Mississippi (Ole Miss), she pursued a Bachelor of Science in Integrated Marketing Communications with a minor in Business.

She graduated from Ole Miss in 2025 and will use her degree and experiences wherever God takes her. Her debut book, *You Are Worthy of New Beginnings*, reflects her unique personal growth through the hardships she has encountered from a young age.

When she's not coaching or writing, Mya enjoys painting with acrylic paint and spending time with her dog and two cats. The inspiration for *You Are Worthy of New Beginnings* came from her desire to encourage and advocate for others through her story.

Through her book, Mya hopes to inspire others to embrace their unique journey. She is excited to see how sharing her story will connect her with readers and open new opportunities along the way.

You can connect with Mya Johnson at myajohnson.com and on Instagram at mya_johnson.14.